I Saw the Muses

Essential Poets Series 71

Leonardo Sinisgalli

I Saw the Muses

Selected Poems: 1931-1942

Edited and translated by Rina Ferrarelli

GUERNICA
Toronto / New York / Lancaster
1997

Original title: *Vidi le muse*

Printed in Canada.

Antonio D'Alfonso, Editor
Guernica Editions Inc.
P.O. Box 117, Station P, Toronto (ON), Canada M5S 2S6
250 Sonwil Drive, Buffalo, New York 14225-5516 U.S.A.
Gazelle, Falcon House, Queen Square, Lancaster LA1 1RN UK

Legal Deposit — First Quarter.
National Library of Canada.
Library of Congress Catalog Card Number: 95-75427

Canada Cataloguing in Publication Data
Sinsigalli, Leonardo, 1908-
I saw the muses : selected poems, 1931-1942
(Essential poets ; 71)
Poems translated from the collection entitled:
Vidi le muse, 1943.
ISBN 1-55071-025-7
I. Ferrarelli, Rina. II. Title. III. Series.
PQ4841.I67V513 1995 851'.912 C95-900167-0

Table of Contents

FIRST POEMS (1931-1937)

ELYSIAN FIELDS (1937-1939)

THE INDIFFERENT HUNTER (1939-1942)

Acknowledgements

Some poems first appeared in the following publications:

Artful Dodge: 'Maybe Even this Memory Is Useless';
Denver Quarterly: 'The Hospital'; 'A Boy Dies a Little'; 'The Bell's Clanging at the End of the Line';
International Poetry Review: 'When Autumn Returns'; 'I Stand Up to the Blast'; 'Passionflower';
Montana Review: 'The Light Was Shouted';
New Letters: 'San Babila'; 'The Sun Will Not Stop'; 'September's New Moon';
Pittsburgh Quarterly: 'See-Through Skins, Souls Light As Air'; 'They'll Burn What Images Bother Them'; 'The Sky's Flickering';
Prism International: 'If a Lizard Stops'; 'To Enjoy the View';
Translation: 'Velasca Avenue'; 'To My Father'; 'Father'; 'I Saw the Muses'; 'The Running Dogs';
Webster Review: 'December at Porta Nuova';
Mid-American Review (VIII/2): Where the Age of the Rose Burned Proudly, a chapbook: 'Dawn is Barely'; 'The Sun Opens'; 'Boys Pitch'; 'Pink, the Muted Pink'; 'Santo Stefano 1941'; 'Elegy I and II'; 'Elysian Fields'; 'Green Leaves'; 'Old Verses'; 'I Know Now Not to Complain.'

First Poems

(1931-1937)

Non si consola di frondi

Non si consola di frondi
Questo corpo d'autunno
Che il vento morde. Nel cavo
Delle ossa la terra preme
Per metter fiore. Prima
Voce (poi chiara un'ala
Che s'apre) la luce è sui rami
deserta. Aggiorna sui tuoi passi.
Ora l'albero è potato
E il suo legame è più saldo
Alla tua legge.

L'aurora appena

L'aurora appena
È uscita dai forni.
Nasce allora dal sonno
Al primo vento
Il lamento delle spighe.
Non più vigile la grazia
Ti cade dalla mano
Falce d'oro. Al suolo
Il seno ti accalora.
La testa in luce prende altura.
Grave ora è la terra
Al sole, forte il sesso.

Green Leaves

Green leaves afford no consolation
to this windbitten autumn body.
To flower the earth presses deep
into the hollow of bones. First a call
(then a bright wing opening) light
is on the branches, forlorn. Day
breaks across your steps.
The tree is pruned now, its ties
to your laws more solid.

Dawn Is Barely

Dawn is barely
out of the oven
when a moan of ripening wheat
rises out of sleep
in the early wind.
You're no longer watchful
and grace falls out of your hand
a golden sickle. On the ground
your breast warms you,
head in relief in the light.
The earth is heavy now
in the sun, sex strong.

Alita fredda la sera

Alita fredda la sera
Su questi prati che toccai con la fronte
Calda e felice della corsa.

Faceva piena nei canali

Faceva piena nei canali
La sera fiorita di eriche
E cresceva fino a toccarti il piede.
Chiamavi l'ultima luce
All'inganno della fonte e la rondine
Il petto molle dei primi
Voli sugli orzi, ti garriva
Nelle vesti.

Ora so non dolermi

Ora so non dolermi
Se la mano nel buio
Tocca il fondo e tu non ci sei.
Allora cercavo la tua ombra
In quella del muro
Sulla terra bianca d'infanzia.
I compagni gridavano a perdifiato
Freschi di capelli nell'afa.
Tu muovevi la polvere dietro le spalle.

The Evening's Breath Cold

The evening's breath cold
on these meadows touched once with a brow
hot and happy from running.

Water Overflowed in the Ditches

Water overflowed in the ditches
the evening blooming with heather
and it swelled all the way to your feet.
You called out to the last light,
the fountain a pretext, and the swallow,
breast wet from its early
flights on the barley, twittered
in your dress.

I Know Now Not to Complain

I know now not to complain
if my hand touches bottom in the dark
and you are not there.
Then, in the white land of childhood,
I searched for your shadow
within the shadow of the wall.
Our friends yelled at the top of their lungs
hair cool in the heat.
You stirred the dust behind them.

A bel vedere sull'aia

A bel vedere sull'aia
tante notti abbiamo dormito,
Le mani affondate nel grano,
Il sonno guardato dai cani.
Più mansueti erano i tuoi piedi
Dei colombi fatti per burla
Col panno bianco dei fazzoletti.
Avevi fili di paglia nei capelli:
Alle spalle muovevi il prato
A una trepida suoneria.

I cani allentano la corsa

I cani allentano la corsa
Tra i pali arsi delle viti.
Così bassa è Orione
Queste sere miti di fine d'anno.
Oscilla il Carro d'oro a questa svolta.
Tu guardi l'alba della luna rossa
Nell'uliveta. La collina è scossa
Da un rumore di frantoio.
Fresca è la ghiaia: sui passi tuoi
La ruota non la spezza.
Perduta alle spalle la fanciullezza
Si fa più lontana, ombra
Cieca nella polvere.

To Enjoy the View

To enjoy the view many nights
we slept on the threshing ground
hands deep in the wheat
sleep-watched by the dogs.
Your feet were meeker
than the pigeons made for fun
with the white cloth of handkerchiefs.
Straw in your hair
you set off a timorous alarm
behind you in the meadow.

The Running Dogs

The running dogs slow down
among the parched grapevine stakes.
Orion is very low
these mild year-end nights.
And around this bend
the golden Great Bear flickers.
You watch the dawning of the red moon
in the olive grove. The hill is shaken
by the sound of an oil-press.
The gravel is cool: the wheel
does not break it in your steps.
Lost behind you, childhood
diminishes in the distance,
blind shadow in the dust.

La luce era gridata

La luce era gridata a perdifiato
Le sere che il sole basso
Arrossava il petto delle rondini rase.
Ora e sempre più viva
Sarà la smania di far notte in me solo
E cercar scampo e riposo
Nella mia storia più remota.
Ogni sera mi vado incontro a ritroso.

L'amico tradito

L'amico tradito mi chiama
Dal fondo del cuore e s'avvicina.
Sento nel sonno che sale.
Io grido all'ultimo passo
Perchè mi calpesti.
Poi mi dorme leggero sul petto.

Caldo com'ero

Caldo com'ero nel tuo alvo
Mi attacco alle tue reni
Madre mia. Io sono
Il tuo frutto e a te ritorno
Ogni notte e nell'ora della morte.
Dormiremo come una volta,
Le mie piante premute
contro il tuo cuore.

The Light Was Shouted

The light was shouted at the top of our lungs
those evenings when the low sun
reddened the breasts of the skimming swallows.
Now and always more alive the longing
to let night fall in me alone
to find escape and rest
in my most remote history.
Every evening I meet myself going back.

The Friend I Betrayed

The friend I betrayed calls me
from deep in my heart, comes near.
I hear him climbing in my sleep.
At the last footfall I scream
that he step on me.
Then he sleeps light on my chest.

Warm As I Was

Warm as I was in your womb,
I cling to your loins,
dear mother. I am
your fruit and I return to you
every night and at the hour of death.
We'll sleep like we did once
the soles of my feet
pressed against your heart.

I fanciulli battono le monete rosse

I fanciulli battono le monete rosse
Contro il muro. (Cadono distanti
Per terra con dolce rumore.) Gridano
A squarciagola in un fuoco di guerra
Si scambiano motti superbi
E dolcissime ingiurie. La sera
Incendia le fronti, infuria i capelli.
Sulle selci calda è come sangue.
Il piazzale torna calmo.
Una moneta battuta si posa
Vicino all'altra alla misura di un palmo.
Il fanciullo preme sulla terra
La sua mano vittoriosa.

Mi difendo a questa raffica

Mi difendo a questa raffica
Che spolvera la luce della piazza
Sulle cime dei pioppi.
Nel debole riverbero uno stormo
Di foglie risale il ciglio della murata.
Batte qui dove mi duole
Questa voce tutta notte:
Mi ritorna la triste
Vocazione ad esistere,
La brama di cercarmi in ogni luogo.

Boys Pitch the Red Coins

Boys pitch the red coins
against the wall. (They fall
far off on the ground
with a soft sound.) Exchanging
proud words and the sweetest insults,
they yell at the top of their lungs
in a heat of battle. Evening,
hot like blood on the cobblestones,
sets fire to their brows, messes their hair.
The square grows calm again.
A pitched coin rests
next to another only a span away.
The boy presses his conquering hand
against the ground.

I Stand Up to the Blast

I stand up to the blast
that sprinkles the tops of the poplars
with the light of the piazza.
In the faint reflection a crowd
of leaves climbs again the top of the wall.
All night this voice
beats here where it hurts:
I get back the sad
vocation to exist
the urge to seek myself everywhere.

In quest'ansa dell'agri

In quest'ansa dell'Agri,
Ai limiti bassi della terra,
Fiduciosa la sera mi consente
La pace casta delle acque.
Di luce arida, un'ala
Che appena turba lo stagno, si avviva
La vena in cuore, fuggitiva.
Torno da pascoli magri
E mi fu cara pena
La faticosa attesa:
Al buio seno ti ascolto
Sera stremata in rive morte.

Eri dritta e felice

Eri dritta e felice
Sulla porta che il vento
Apriva alla campagna.
Intrisa di luce
Stavi ferma nel giorno,
Al tempo delle vespe d'oro
Quando al sambuco
Si fanno dolci le midolla.
Allora s'andava scalzi
Per i fossi, si misurava l'ardore
Del sole dalle impronte
Lasciate sui sassi.

At this Bend of the River

At this bend of the river
at the low edge of the earth,
trusting, evening grants me
the chaste peace of a stream.
Arid of light, a wing
barely disturbing a pond, the fleeting
vein quickens in my heart.
I'm back from lean pastures
where the waiting
was hard, bittersweet.
I'm listening to your dark breast,
evening, as you lie exhausted
on these dead shores.

You Stood Straight and Happy

You stood straight and happy
at the door the wind
opened to the countryside.
Drenched in light
poised in the day,
at the time of golden wasps
when the elder's marrow
sweetens.
We walked barefoot
through the ditches then,
we measured the sun's
heat by the prints
left on the rocks.

Il sole ti apre

Il sole ti apre la mano superba
E la noia del giorno
Prende un calore carnale.
L'albero ha rotto i legami dell'aria.
La terra ne è tutta partecipe.
Disseminata è la luce
Per crescere sulle pietre.
La bestia assapora la rara erba.

Sono a questa riva

Sono a questa riva e mi chiama
Il suono del giorno ch'io ruppi
A sassate. La luce nuova è aperta
Sulla terra che calpesto
E nulla è ancora più giovane
Delle mie ossa. L'estate arde
Sulle stoppie. Senza rumore
Si sgretola entro il mio corpo
Questo fuoco.

The Sun Opens

The sun opens your proud hand
and the day's boredom
takes on the heat of flesh.
The tree has broken its ties with the air
and the earth knows all about it.
The light's scattered like seed
to grow upon rocks.
The beast of the field
savors the rare grass.

I Stand on this Bank

I stand on this bank, the sound
of the day that I broke with rocks
beckoning me. The new light
is open on the earth I trample
and nothing yet is younger
than my bones. Summer burns
across the stubble. Without a sound
this fire
crumbles within my body.

A mani aperte mi fa giorno

A mani aperte mi fa giorno
E l'alba indugia a sollevarsi
Come una vela fresca sul mio corpo
E il sangue è felice e mi corre
La brezza, mi cresce mattina sul mare.
Nel dormiveglia le voci della regata
Hanno cadenze di estrema avventura.
L'acqua è un prato sotto i piedi
Fiorita, la luce dentro le mani
È fredda come un'unghia.

Finisce qui una giornata

Finisce qui una giornata
Al vento che rannuvola la vasca.
Chiara una voce dal fondo chiama
La rana o questa luna che rinasce.
In bisce nell'acqua verde
Ecco l'infanzia inquieta
Che riaffiora luminosa a mani lisce.
L'ombra non si perde nella mota,
Così nitida è stasera
La rete vuota in fondo alla peschiera.

Day Breaks in Me

Day breaks in me with open hands
and dawn rises slowly
like a cool sail over my body
and my blood is happy and a breeze
blows, a morning on the sea
grows in me. When I'm half asleep
the sounds of the regatta
have the cadence of high adventure.
In bloom, the water is a meadow
underfoot, the light in my hands
cold as a fingernail.

A Day Comes to an End

A day comes to an end
in the wind darkening the tank.
A clear voice or this new-born moon
calls the frog from the bottom.
Among snakes in the green water
my restless childhood
resurfacing now luminous with smooth hands.
Its shadow is not lost in the mud,
the empty net so clear, tonight,
at the bottom of the fishpond.

San Babila

Trascina il vento della sera
Attaccate agli ombrelli a colore
Le piccole fioraie
Che strillano gaie nelle maglie.
Come rondini alle grondaie
Resteranno sospese nell'aria
Le venditrici di dalie
Ora che il vento della sera
Gonfia gli ombrelli a mongolfiera.

San Babila

The evening wind drags along
the little flowergirls
hanging from many-colored umbrellas,
squealing gaily in their sweaters.
Like swallows under the eaves
they will stay suspended in mid-air
the dahlia vendors
now that the evening wind
swells the umbrellas into balloons.

Elegia I

Mi ricorderò di questo autunno
Splendido e fugitivo dalla luce migrante
Curva al vento sul dorso delle canne.
La piena dei canali è salita alla cintura
E mi ci sono immerso disseccato dalla siccità.
Quando sarò con gli amici nelle notti di città
Farò la storia di questi giorni di ventura
Di mio padre che a pestar l'uva
S'era fatti i piedi rossi
Di mia madre timorosa
Che porta un uovo caldo nella mano
Ed è più felice d'una sposa.
Mio padre parlava di quel ciliegio
Piantato il giorno delle nozze, mi diceva,
Quest'anno non ha avuto fioritura,
e sognava di farne il letto nuziale a me primogenito.
Il vento di tramontana apriva il cielo
Al quarto di luna. La luna coi corni
Rosei, appena spuntati, di una vitella!
Domani si potrà seminare, diceva mio padre.
Sul palmo aperto della mano guardavo
i solchi chiari contro il fuoco, io sentivo
Scoppiare il seme nel suo cuore,
Io vedevo nei suoi occhi fiammeggiare
La conca spigata.

Elegy I

I'll remember this splendid
and fleeting autumn, the migrant light
bent in the wind on the back of the canes.
The water in the canals swelled to my waist
and parched by drought I sank into it.
On city nights, among friends,
I'll tell the story of these serendipitous days
of my father whose feet turned red
stomping grapes, of my timid mother
who carries a warm egg in her hand
and is happier than a bride.
My father, speaking of that cherry tree
planted on his wedding day, said,
It hasn't bloomed this year,
and dreamed of making
a nuptial bed for me, his firstborn.
The north wind opens the sky
to a quarter moon — the moon
with the pink, barely sprouted horns of a heifer!
Tomorrow we can sow, my father said.
Against the fire I looked at the clear
furrows on his open palm, I heard
the seed burst in his heart
I saw flashing in his eyes
the ripening fields.

Elegy II

Dolce compagno dove sei? I rami
Degli alberi gemelli intrecciano
In nitide ombre le linee
delle nostre due vite sulla terra.
Io ti cerco come Ulisse cercava i suoi compagni
Nel porcaio. Il guardiano mi dice:
Non t'inganni il colore, il porco nero
occùpa, il porco bianco fa più lume.
Ma il mio occhio è stanco e poco sagace.
Io non sono più astuto come un tempo
Ero con te furbo mercante ai giuochi.
Se la luna potesse spargere, questa sera,
Per un attimo solo, sui miei porci bianchi
E neri come rondini il miele di Circe
Ti ritroverei mio compagno dai denti forti.
Ti racconterei le gioie di quest'inverno
Di provincia, trascorso nelle terre della nostra
Infanzia. Ho toccato con la mia mano
la ferita aperta nel fianco della volpe,
Ho cacciato dalla tana la mia solitudine.
Dionisio torna ancora alle nostre feste
E le donne sbattono i campani
per cacciare il capro dalle selve.
Io ti cerco nei pozzi chiari questa sera
Come allora che nel corpo dipinto delle rane
Si cercavano i nostri morti.

Elegy II

My gentle friend, where are you? The branches
of twin trees braid in clear shadows
the lines of our two lives on earth.
I look for you in the pigsty, as Ulysses
did his mates. The keeper says:
Don't be deceived by the color, the black pig
makes it darker, the white, gives off light.
But my eyes are tired and not very sharp.
I'm not as shrewd as I used to be, when you and I
were like cunning hucksters at our games.
If, tonight, the moon could spread,
for one instant only, Circe's honey
on my pigs black and white like swallows,
I would find you again, friend of the strong teeth.
I would tell you the joy of this winter
spent away from the city, in the land of our childhood.
I've touched with my own hand
the open wound in the fox's side,
I've chased loneliness from its den.
Dionisius still comes to our festivals
and the women bang the heavy bells
to chase the buck out of the woods.
I look for you in the clear wells tonight
as we used to look for our dead
in the spotted bodies of frogs.

Dicembre a Porta Nuova

Mi raccoglie nel suo gomito
Inerte la fredda sera d'autunno.
Scorre deserta sulle foglie
E mi ridesta a ogni tonfo
Dei castagni. Tutto il bene
Che mi resta forse è in quest'ora
Calma che si accerta,
A questa svolta che si gonfia
D'acque perchè la ripa si fa stretta.
Poi rotta la dolcezza dell'indugio
Ogni cosa decade con più fretta
E non mi duole l'alito d'ombra
Che mi gela la fronte.
Sopra la spalletta curvo
Mi assale il vento dalla buca del ponte.

December at Porta Nuova

The cold fall evening gathers me
inert in the crook of its arm,
flows deserted over the leaves
awakening me with each thud
from the chestnut trees.
All the good left me may be
in this calm hour I can be certain of
at this bend swelling with water
between narrowing banks.
Then once the tender pause is over
everything decays rapidly
and I no longer mind the breath
of shadow chilling my forehead.
As I bend over the rail the wind
rushes at me from under the bridge.

Narni-Amelia Scalo

I ricordi li cancelli questa sera
Che un nome nuovo ti solleva la fatica
E una data scritta sopra la lavagna.
Sostano in mezzo alla campagna
I convogli dei treni merci.
Poi girano lentamente sul ponte della Nera.
T'è lontana la voce lungo i nastri
Trasportatori, straniera la terra
Distesa sotto la tettoia.
Ti sembra che ogni guerra
Si concluda in una resa e che ti valga
Per la tua povera gioia
La docile sorpresa dei tuoi astri
Familiari in un cielo d'esilio.
È un'ora buona per te e questi allarmi
Di campanelle nel fumo non ti dolgono.
Aspetti che risalga
Il secchio dalla stridula cisterna.
Oscillano nell'oscura fuligine i vetri rossi
Della lanterna. Tu senti che è primavera
Da queste ventate di meli scossi
Dai treni lungo la pianura.

Narni-Amelia Freight Yard

You erase your memories tonight
when a new name relieves your weariness
and a date written on the board.
Convoys of freight trains
stop in the middle of the fields
then move slowly across the Nera river bridge.
Distant the voice along the conveyor
belts, foreign the land
stretched under the roof.
You feel that every war ends
in surrender, but it's enough
for your meager joy
the mild surprise of familiar stars
in a sky of exile.
These are good times and you don't mind
the warning bells in the smoke.
You wait for the bucket
to come up the shrill cistern.
The red panes of the lantern
swing in the dark mist. You know it's spring
from the whiffs of apple trees shaken
by the trains across the moor.

Lazzaretto

Sul gambo teso è sazio il girasole.
Così il peso del giorno è in questo poco
Spazio di terra, fresca
Tomba alle membra, gremita
D'ombra che mi oscura la via
Dove tornerò sempre.
La sera mi porta lungo la muraglia
Ancora un riverbero fioco
Di quella perduta forza,
E ha un ritorno d'allegria
Sui bordi del prato il fuoco
Che stizza le labili liste di paglia.

Verdesca

Per anni mi soccorse la tua vista,
Dolce compagno, quella che ricordo
Fu la rissa sul ponte. Maggio
Ha le sere stordite, io non volli
Vederti che di spalle, dietro i rami
Rapito nella corsa.
Poi ti ho perduto è ancora nel miraggio
Ti rincorro estenuato sulla pista
Del giorno che ti rotola nel cerchio.
Da allora ogni bene mi è stato soverchio.

The Hospital

On the taut stem the sated sunflower
thus the weight of the day in this small
patch of earth, cool
grave for my limbs, crowded
with the shadow that darkens the street
where I always go back.
Along the wall
the evening brings me still
a flicker of that lost strength,
and at the edge of the meadow
cheerful again the fire
that vexes the fleeting straws.

Verdesca

For years the sight of you helped me,
dear friend. What I remember
is the fight on the bridge. Evenings
are dazed in May, I wanted to see
only your back, through the branches
as you ran and ran.
Then I lost you and in the mirage
I'm still chasing you
worn out on the track of the day
that winds you in its circle.
Every good since then has been a plus.

Elysian Field

(1937-1939)

Toute l'année j'ai tripoté d'après nature . . .
Cependant encore une fois je me laisse aller
à faire des étoiles trop grandes . . .

Van Gogh

Campi Elisi

Di là dalla dolce provincia dell'Agri
Siete approdati alle rive sognate,
Oscuri morti familiari.
Le vostre salme hanno dato salute
Al verde degli orti.
I campi di fave si sono allargati
Oltre i cancelli:
Dove arse superba l'età delle rose
Le capre pestano la terra
Nei giorni di siccità.

Via Velasca

Il calpestio di tanti anni
L'ha quasi affondata, la via
Incredibilmente si è stretta.
Questa è l'ora mia, la mia ora diletta.
Io ricordo la sera che alla fioca
Luce si spense ogni rumore, un grido
Disse il mio nome come in sogno e sparve.
La via s'incurva, sgocciola
Il giorno dalle cime dei tetti:
Quest'ora dolce suona nel petto.
Non è che una larva restia
La luce, un barlume: entro la boccia
Di vetro un pesce s'illumina.

Elysian Fields

They've landed beyond the mild
region of the Agri river
at the shores they longed for,
these obscure family dead.
Their bodies have given well-being
to the gardens' green.
The horsebean fields have spread
past the gates:
where the age of the rose burned proudly
goats pound the earth
in times of drought.

Velasca Avenue

Almost sunk by all the years
of trampling, the street
has incredibly narrowed.
This is my hour, my favorite hour.
I remember the evening when in the dim light
every noise ceased, as in a dream
a shout said my name and faded away.
The street curves, the day
drips from the rooftops:
this quiet hour strikes in the breast.
Only a restless ghost
the light, a glimmer: a fish
kindles in the glass bowl.

A perdita d'occhi

Non tarderà a far giorno,
L'umidore è già sulla tua fronte
E sulle foglie il ragno stende
I fili perchè debole in giro
Con la punta d'un'ala
Appena la luce si bagni.
S'agita l'erba al tuo respiro, spunta
Il sole che tocchi: col piede
Distendi l'orizzonte a perdita d'occhi.

Contro il muro dell'orto

Contro il muro dell'orto
Teso come un velo
Azzurro nella sera
La cara ombra si accosta
Assorta. Trema sul fianco
Della collina Espero
E s'avvicina a schiarire le frondi.
Un dolce incanto la tiene
Viva nell'aria mossa.
Ecco l'ombra si arrossa.
Ecco cade il mio cielo.

As Far As the Eye Can See

Soon it will be day,
your forehead is damp, and the spider
stretches its threads on the leaves
so that the weak light circling
will only bathe
with the tip of a wing.
The grass stirs at your breath, the sun
you touch rises: with your foot
you stretch the horizon as far as the eye can see.

Against the Garden Wall

Against the garden wall
taut like a blue veil
in the night, her dear shadow
approaches, rapt.
On the slope of the hill
the evening star flickers,
draws near to shine on the leaves.
A sweet magic keeps her
alive in the shimmering air.
The shadow reddens now.
My sky falls now.

Passiflora

È nostro ancora questo fioco
Lume della sera, un barbaglio
Sulle cime dei lecci. Il fuoco
Nella stanza si consuma; (un sommesso
brusio disperde la tua vigilanza)
e appena ti lambisce svampa
La veste: un ardore
Ti difende dalla fiamma come la foglia
Sempreverde. Tremi
Ora che gli orti
Devasta la tramontana
E ne patisce dietro i vetri lividi
La pigra passiflora.

Strenua tu canti

Strenua tu canti
Su questa piazza in rovina
Da una foglia di platano, tu sola
Viva nell'aria crepitante.
È l'ora che invisa splende
Bianca la Canicola.
Ma dalle mura sfinestrate
Voci remote di fanciulli
Fan ressa. Il fumo nell'afa
Le dissolve. I cani non dan tregua
alla donnola uscita dalla polvere.

Passionflower

Still ours this faint
evening light, a glimmer
in the holly tops. The fire
burns on in the room, a low
buzzing scatters your attention,
and as soon as it grazes you
your dress kindles: an ardor
protects you and the evergreen leaf
from the flame. You shiver
now that the north wind
ravages the gardens
and behind the livid panes
the numb passionflower suffers.

Tirelessly You Sing

Tirelessly you sing
from a sycamore leaf
above the piazza in ruin, only you
alive in the crackling air.
It's the time when the hated
Dog Star shines white.
But from the gouged windows in the walls
distant voices of children
crowd each other out. Smoke
dissolves them in the heat. The dogs
give no respite to the weasel
emerging from the dust.

Genova

Sempre che torni sera
Per queste città dove le luci
Appena si staccano dai pali
E il mare brucia di là
Sul molo un'aria fiacca
Raccoglie il fischio della sirena.
Solo mi dico la mia pena e brillano
Agli occhi vaghi i lumi delle ville.
Troppo dolce il passaggio in queste terre,
Più sicura la morte, ad ogni viaggio
Non c'è speranza che resti sepolta.
Poi è la prima stella che si perde
Dietro le palme, più tardi un baleno
Verde che s'apre a uno schiocco di frusta.

Sera di San Lorenzo

Mi rialzo alle colline
(Così lustre di pula lenta nel soffio d'agosto)
Silvestro, dolce amico, mi rassegni
D'ogni cosa trascorsa, dell'usura
Che fa liscia la pietra sopra il grano,
E una foglia mi porgi sulla mano
generosa. Nel torpido alone
Della giovane luna ti chiudi
E parli di tante allegrie.
Fresco il vento sugli occhi si avviva
E rintoccano i sonagli alle vette.
Sono luci di San Lorenzo
Le fole che vidi ardere: tu ridi
Se penso la fila lunga
Di formiche che bruci.

Genoa

Always when day turns into dusk
in these cities where the lights
cling to their poles and the sea blazes nearby
the siren's wail gathers
in the languid air of the pier.
Alone I speak my pain as the lights
of the villas shine in my unfocused eyes.
Too mild the passage through these lands,
death is more certain, with each trip
less hope that it will stay buried.
Then it is the first star that disappears
behind the palms, a green flash later
that opens at the crack of a whip.

Night of the Shooting Stars

I climb the shimmering hills again,
the chaff softly-blown in the August wind,
and you Sylvester, my dear friend,
bring me up to date on what's happened,
on how stone wears smooth grinding wheat,
and you offer me a leaf
on your generous hand. Then shut
within the young moon's torpid halo,
you talk of all the fun you've had.
The cool wind freshens across our eyes
and the cowbells ring in the hilltops.
The fantasies I saw blazing
are shooting stars: you laugh
if I think long
the line of ants you burn.

Se una lucertola si ferma

Le dolci acque fumano
Nella calura stasera. Sono
Senza peso e senza pena.
Il mio cuore giace sulla tiepida
Paglia. Mia madre su quest'aia
Ha battuto la mazza.

Rue Sainte Walburge

Forse ha battuto più forte
il tuo cuore dei tacchi del lanciere.
Ti ritorna il frastuono in un odore
di capelli, i giorni belli
al moto biondo della Mosa.
Sbiadiscono nella caligine
la strada del borgo, le scritte
straniere delle insegne, i campi
dietro le palafitte.
Tu ne ritrovi la traccia
E da uno sbuffo di vapore
avanza la cara figura d'amore
quei dolci tacchi battuti sul cuore
e l'ombra calda sulla faccia.

If a Lizard Stops

The gentle stream smokes
in the heat tonight. I'm without
burdens and without pain,
my heart lying on the warm
straw. My mother swung a flail
on this threshing ground.

Rue Sainte Walburge

Maybe your heart beat louder
than a lancer's boots.
A scent of hair brings back
the din, the Meuse's blond
flowing the sunny days.
The road to town, the foreign language
signs, the fields behind the pilings
fade in the mist.
You find again their trace
and from a puff of vapor
the image of your love walks toward you
those gentle heels beating on your heart
her shadow warm on your face.

Santo Stefano 1938

Stasera s'indovina al chiaro delle nevi
Che il giorno avanza con passi di gallo.
Dalla mia stanza erta
Guardo il ballo delle ombre nel solstizio.
C'è nell'aria un indizio
Di vita nuova, una speranza certa.
Forse è il cuore che smania
In questa bianca squilla remota
O il vento che si stana.
Tra lo stridore delle pale il giorno
Vuoto è scacciato, un anno s'allontana.
La luna tardi splenderà sul selciato.

La luna nuova di settembre

La luna nuova di settembre
ha cacciato i ragazzi sulla via.
Soffiano nelle mani, un po' vili
un po' pazzi, rifanno il verso
alla puzzola che si duole.
Ruzzolan nei cortili
tra i rovi e i calcinacci
a far razzia.
Hanno le ali ai piedi,
stringono le uova calde nelle tasche.
Li asseconda la luna che addormenta
i guardiani sulle frasche.

Santo Stefano 1938

Tonight one can make out in the light of snow
that the day advances like a strutting rooster.
From my steep room
I look at the dance of shadows in the solstice.
In the air is a trace
of something new, a sure hope.
Maybe it's my heart delirious
in this white remote pealing
or the wind leaving its den.
In the din of shovels, the empty
day is driven away, a year moves on.
The moon will shine late on the pavement.

September's New Moon

September's new moon
has driven the boys out on the street.
They blow on their hands, now cowardly
now wild, mimic
the hurt weasel's cry.
Bent on piracies
they tumble in the yards
in the briars and mortar chunks.
With winged heels they flee
holding tight in their pockets the warm eggs.
The moon favors them
by putting the watchmen to sleep
on the branches.

Padre mio

Padre mio che sei
sulla loggia dopo cena
e sonnecchi. Ti scuoti
al rumore dell'acqua
che dal barile è calata nei secchi.
Anna innaffia la terra
delle fucsie materne.
Poi con la mano ti scaccia
i moscerini dalla faccia.

Vidi le muse

Sulla collina
Io certo vidi le Muse
Appollaiate tra le foglie.
Io vidi allora le Muse
Tra le foglie larghe delle querce
Mangiare ghiande e coccole.
Vidi le Muse su una quercia
secolare che gracchiavano.
Meravigliato il mio cuore
Chiesi al mio cuore meravigliato
Io dissi al mio cuore la meraviglia.

Father

Father, you sit
on the balcony after supper
and doze. You stir
at the sound of water pouring
from the barrel into the can.
Anna waters the earth
around mother's fuchsias.
Then she chases
the gnats off your face
with her hand.

I Saw the Muses

I'm sure I saw the Muses
on the hill
roosting among the leaves.
I saw then the Muses
eating acorns and berries
among the wide oak leaves.
I saw the Muses croaking
on an ancient oak.
My heart marveling
I asked my marveling heart
I told my heart the marvel.

The Indifferent Hunter

(1939-1942)

Quando torna l'autunno

Quando torna l'autunno si fa tenera
La terra nei piazzali, la sera
Lunga al grido del venditore
D'erba corallina.
Sulla collina si accendono i fuochi:
È l'ora propizia ai giuochi.
Tu entri nel labirinto col piede
Leggero come un piede dipinto.
Questa traccia esitante senza fine
È la tua sorte; se passi il confine
La morte può cogliere nel segno.
Non lo sapevi tu re
Delle nostre sere segrete, lucifero
Nel nostro regno?
La tua ombra è rimasta nella rete,
Il tuo piede legato
Alla staffa del cavallo fulminato.

Una pioggia di cenere, il bagliore

Una pioggia di cenere, il bagliore
Dei fari sulle piante semprevive
Questa sera. Più tenera ti serra
La querela di parole perdute
A un caro braccio, a un'ombra
Che t'avvinca. Al buio
Stenti a trovare la traccia
D'una strada sepolta, e una pervinca
Nel fumo della nebbia, raso
Terra una luce pungente
spunta ai bordi del salvagente.

When Autumn Returns

When autumn returns, the ground's
tender in the clearings, the evening long
in the cry of the vendor selling greens.
Erba corallina.
On the hill fires are lit:
the time is right for games.
You enter the maze your foot as light
as a foot in a painting.
This endless hesitant track
is your destiny; if you cross the border
death might find its mark.
Did you not know it king
of our secret evenings, our kingdom's
morning star?
Your shadow stayed behind in the net,
the horse struck by lightning,
your foot stuck in the stirrup.

A Rain of Ashes, the Glare

A rain of ashes, the glare
of headlights on the evergreens
tonight. And more tenderly binding
the complaining words lost
to a loving arm, to a shadow
who'd clasp you. In the dark
you barely find the trace
of a buried street, and a periwinkle
in the smoke of fog. Close to the ground
a stinging light appears
at the edge of the traffic island.

Spuntano gemme dai salici

Spuntano gemme dai salici appena
Estinta è la luna di dicembre.
Di là dal colle non potrai tornare
In quest'aria delusa, sulla breccia
Che luce come il sale.

Strepita la campana

Strepita la campana al capolinea.
La tramontana spazza contro il fiume
La polvere delle case in rovina.
Eccoti sola e la piazza ti sperde
Al bivio, e tu non sai
Più vivere, non sai dimenticare.
Era verde il sambuco quella sera,
Freschi i tumuli di terra
Fuori della città lungo il declivio
Che da Santa Sabina
Scende a Bocca della Verità.
Ahi, ahi, stravolta (oggi l'anno ci coglie
Così distanti per strade traverse)
Tu cammini, io ti chiamo. Alle finestre
Scroscia a sghembo la pioggia.
E ti sollevi l'ammasso di capelli
Dagli orecchi, scrolli
I perduti ricordi: una nube
Di corvi dal mio cielo
S'è posata stasera nel tuo specchio.

Willows Burst into Bud

Willows burst into bud as soon
as December's moon has waned.
You can't go back beyond the hill
in this air awash with regret, on the gravel
that shines like salt.

The Bell's Clanging

The bell's clanging at the end of the line.
The north wind sweeps against the river
the dust of the houses in ruin.
Suddenly you are alone and the piazza
loses you at the crossroads.
You no longer know how to live
no longer know how to forget.
The elder was green that evening
fresh the mounds of earth
outside the city along the slope
that goes from Santa Sabina
to Bocca della Verità.
Distraught (the year finds us today
far apart on parallel streets)
you walk away, I call to you. Rain
slants hard against the windowpanes.
You lift the heavy hair
from your ears, shake
the lost memories: a cloud
of ravens from my sky
has lit in your mirror tonight.

Santo Stefano 1941

Calpestiamo le foglie morte
Sull'una e l'altra riva
Il fiume è tiepido come cenere
Se lo tocchi. Pare
Che scenda profondamente
Dentro la terra il cielo
In queste chiare notti di guerra.

Da quanti anni, da sempre

Da quanti anni, da sempre
Sul finire del giorno
Lungo il muro il tuo passo ritorna
La tua mano mi tocca
Delusa: Leonardo, mi dici a bocca
Chiusa. Il vento leggera ti scioglie.
Io ti sento partire dal mio fianco
Nella brezza delle foglie.
La tua voce è una carezza
Che brucia più l'ora si attarda:
Io non so dove mi conduce.

Santo Stefano 1941

We trample dead leaves
first on one then on the other bank
the river warm like ashes
to the touch. The sky
these clear nights of war
seems to plunge deep into the earth.

How Many Years, Now, Since Always

How many years, now, since always
at the end of the day
your steps return along the wall
your hand touches me
disappointed: Leonardo, you say, mouth
closed. So light the wind dissolves you.
I can feel you leave my side
in the breeze of foliage.
Your voice is a caress that burns
more deeply as the hour grows late.
I don't know where it takes me.

I vecchi versi tornano a memoria

Ecco mi alletta
La storia di una rosa
Che la neve cancella (e un segno
Vivo, la brace della tua sigaretta).
Ecco son persi nel buio
Gli ombrelli di Trinità dei Monti.
Se i nostri passi saranno profondi
Avremo pace in un regno
Dove nessuno ci aspetta.

Ogni sera la mano è più leggera

Ogni sera la mano è più leggera
Il volo della rondine è più alto.
Qui rimane lo strepito, il tuo riso
Come un'ala fuggiasca
E l'odore di fulmine più ricco
Del profumo di rose ai davanzali.
Di là qualcosa, un fuoco, ti rapina
Il tuo nido di fuoco all'orizzonte,
il tuo grido . . .

Old Verses Come to Mind

Look, I'm taken by the story of a rose
erased by snow (a living sign
your cigarette's burning tip).
Look, the umbrellas on the Spanish Steps
climb out of sight in the dark.
If our steps sink deep
we'll find peace in a kingdom
where no one's waiting for us.

Every Night Your Hand

Every night your hand grows lighter
the swallow's flight higher.
The rumbling is what's left, your laughter
like a fleeing wing,
and the scent of lightning
richer than the perfume of roses
on the windowsills.
Out there something, a fire, plunders
your nest of fire on the horizon,
your cry . . .

Muore il ragazzo un poco

Muore il ragazzo un poco
ogni giorno per giuoco.
Per giuoco morde invano
Il cavo della mano.
Trascorre le vacanze ebbro
Tra i maceri cespi di papaveri
Steso sul letto per noia
E diletto a guardare le travi.
Ma lo stornano ombre
Solitarie nel cielo della stanza,
Labili ombre passeggere
Sul soffitto. È l'Ariete
Che batte ostinato le corna
A capofitto nella quiete.

A Boy Dies a Little

A boy dies a little
every day in play.
In play he bites in vain
the hollow of his hand.
Drunken with life
he spends his summers
on mashed poppy stalks
on the bed staring at the rafters
out of boredom and delight.
But lonely shadows
in the sky of the room
scatter his attention
fleeting shadows
on the ceiling. It's the Ram
stubbornly pounding his horns
headlong in the stillness.

Dove latra leggera

Dove latra leggera l'anima dei cani
E il grido del fanciullo si tende al guizzo
della fionda, e di tutto il giorno è vano
Ogni altro segno (questa vena grossa
Sul dorso della mano), il 14 luglio
Sono sceso nel regno dei morti, tra i gatti
E le pernici che fan festa sotto i tavoli.
Resterà in queste parole l'ebbrezza
Della mosca nel sole, l'occhio
Del cacciatore indifferente?

Tarquinia, 1940

Bruceranno le immagini moleste

Bruceranno le immagini moleste (la cagna
Bianca sulla cenere dei forni, le bugie
Sotto le ascelle, gli anni belli sulla nuca,
Il lezzo delle fave calpestate dai cavalli).
Bruceranno i ricordi tra i capelli che tu amavi.

Civitavecchia, 1940

Where the Souls of Dogs Bark Softly

Where the souls of dogs bark softly
and the boy's shout leans into
the slingshot's snap, and every other
sign of the day is useless (this swollen vein
on the back of my hand), on July 14
I went down into the realm of the dead, among
the cats and snipes partying under the tables.
Will the ecstacy of a fly in the sun,
the eye of the indifferent hunter
remain in these words?

Tarquinia, 1940

They'll Burn What Images Bother Them

They'll burn what images bother them (the white
bitch on the ash of ovens, the lies under the armpits,
the good years on the nape of the neck,
the stench of broadbeans trampled by horses).
They'll burn the memories with the hair you loved.

Civitavecchia, 1940

Ecco vacilla il cielo

Ecco vacilla il cielo, le stelle
vive come capre tra i cespugli
La primavera scuote il lezzo
Pungente dei pantani. Ogni cosa
È talmente sicura di esistere
Questa notte, in questo canto
Di vecchia rana ad Abbasanta.

1941

The Sky's Flickering

The sky's flickering, now, the stars
frisky as goats in the bushes.
Spring shakes loose the stench
of dead water. Every thing
is so sure to exist tonight, in the song
of this old frog, in Abbasanta.

1941

Naia noia

1
Sei così scaltro nell'attesa
Paziente. Annusi
La terra che fuma, la vita
Che una sigaretta consuma
Lentamente. Niente altro.

2
La dolcezza testarda dei tuoi anni,
L'aprile brullo, un corvo
Fermo sulla garritta,
E le lettere scritte a sera tarda.
Forse la vita è bella . . .
In quell'inferno là in fondo alla via,
Alla pioggia, alla noia, in quell'odore
Di carbonella sotto la tettoia
Della nera mascalcìa.

3
Un tenero abisso si apriva al mio lato.
Quasi sotto i miei piedi una stella
Cadde in un pianto dirotto.

1941

Army Drab

1
How clever you are as you wait
patiently. You sniff
the smoking earth, life
slowly consumed
by a cigarette. Nothing else.

2
The stubborn gentleness of youth,
a bare April, a crow
motionless on the sentry box,
and the letters written late at night.
Maybe life is beautiful . . .
in that inferno at the end of the street,
of rain, boredom, in the smell
of charcoal under the smithy's roof.

3
A tender abyss opened beside me.
Almost underfoot a star
fell to weeping helplessly.

1941

O spoglie trasparenti, o anime leggere!

O spoglie trasparenti, o anime leggere!
Cresce il granturco più alto di voi,
Soffiano i buoi per gli oscuri pantani
Amici fulvi, bai, sauri, roani.
Sono piegati i vessilli. La polvere
Scorre sul filo delle vecchie spade, le stelle
Spuntano in cima alle aste
Immobili ai freddi cancelli.
Le folte criniere, le rosse gambe, i ferri,
Le fruste non fanno scintille.
Una talpa è sbucata nella corte:
Come una vampa nera
S'è richiusa sotterra.

1942

Forse è vano anche questo ricordo

Forse è vano anche questo ricordo
Appena vivo per un fischio
Del ragazzo scomparso
Dietro le mura del borgo
Una mattina di nevischio.
Avevi la testa bendata
Rosso angelo litigioso,
Ti spuntava un'umida rosa
di sangue sotto la garza.
Io ti persi lungo le rampe
Delle mura. Ora non vedo
Che la tua ombra sulla neve
Azzurra, il lume delle tue gambe.

See-Through Skins, Souls Light As Air!

See-through skins, souls light as air!
The corn grows taller than you,
the oxen puff through the dark bogs
my tawny friends, bay, sorrel, roan.
We've folded the flags. Dust
runs on the edge of old swords, the stars
come out on top of the poles
motionless by the cold gates.
Thick manes, red legs, shoes,
whips strike no sparks.
A mole crawls out in the courtyard:
like a black flame
dives underground again.

1942

Maybe Even this Memory Is Useless

Maybe even this memory is useless,
barely alive because of a whistle.
The boy disappeared behind
the town's walls that morning
in the blinding snow, head
bandaged, a moist rose of blood
blooming under the gauze,
a red scrappy angel.
I lost you on the ramps
along the walls. Now I see
only your shadow on the blue
snow, the light of your legs.

Imitazione della luna

La luna sanguina alle corna, mite
Settembre torna ai davanzali.
Ai davanzali una voce balbetta:
Luna, luna nuova
Chi ti cerca non ti trova
Chi ti trova non ti aspetta.
Luna mia alta dove
È il gatto riverso che si spulcia?
Io non lo cerco altrove, luna
Amorosa. Bruciano
Gli occhi al buio, brucia
La tuberosa di settembre luna
Sempre dolorosa.

Rosei del rosa dolce delle case

Rosei del rosa dolce delle case
D'autunno i muratori sopra i tetti
All'aria cantano stretti sull'anca
Docile il piede bianco alle cimase.
Stanno nel cielo in bilico e la voce
Resta sospesa sopra le grondaie
Leggera, che la voce resta in aria.

Imitation of the Moon

The moon's horns are bleeding, mild
September returns to the windowsills.
At the windowsills a voice stammers:
Moon, moon so new
whoever looks cannot find you
whoever finds you
does not want you.
My high high moon, where
is the upside down cat
that picks its fleas?
I won't look for it elsewhere,
lover moon. Eyes burn
in the dark and the tuberose
always sorrowful September moon.

Pink, the Muted Pink of Houses

Pink, the muted pink of houses,
roofers sing in the air in the fall
narrow in the hip, white foot
tame on the ridges. They're balanced
in the sky, and their voices
remain in mid-air, thin,
suspended above the eaves.

Ascolta la voce del maestro

Ascolta la voce del Maestro
La domanda che resta senza risposta
Ecco il gesso, ecco l'unghia che stride
E scrive un nome sulla lavagna.
Sembrano voci di un altro regno
Le dolci voci dei compagni.
Il ragazzo è solo nascosto
Tra le ortiche delle tombe.
Spreme in pugno il veleno d'ogni foglia.
Ha voglia di morire. E uno squillo
Di tromba lo accarezza, un richiamo
Forte come un nitrito.
Riassapora l'inchiostro sulle dita:
E il Maestro che suona?

Listen to the Teacher's Voice

Listen to the teacher's voice
the question still without answer
here's the chalk, the fingernail
that screeching writes a name on the board.
They seem like voices from another kingdom
our classmates' soft voices.
The boy is alone hidden
in the nettles of the graves.
He squeezes in his fist
the poison of every leaf.
He wants to die. And the blare
of a horn caresses him, a call
loud as a neigh. He tastes again
the ink on his fingers:
Is it the teacher who's calling?

A mio padre

L'uomo che torna solo
A tarda sera dalla vigna
Scuote le rape nella vasca
Sbuca dal viottolo con la paglia
Macchiata di verderame.
L'uomo che porta così fresco
Terriccio sulle scarpe, odore
Di fresca sera nei vestiti
Si ferma a una fonte, parla
Con l'ortolano che sradica i finocchi.
E un uomo, un piccolo uomo
Ch'io guardo di lontano.
E un punto vivo all'orizzonte.
Forse la sua pupilla
Si accende questa sera
Accanto alla peschiera
Dove si asciuga la fronte.

Il sole non si fermerà

Un'altra mano alla finestra
farà girare il macinino,
il sole non si fermerà.

To My Father

The man who comes back
alone from the vineyard
late in the evening
shakes the turnips in the trough
emerges from the narrow path
straw hat spotted with verdigris.
The man who wears such fresh
loam on his shoes, the smell
of cool evening on his clothes,
stops at a fountain,
talks with the gardener
who's uprooting fennel.
A man, a small man
whom I watch from a distance.
A live point on the horizon.
Maybe tonight
his eyes will kindle
next to the fishpond
where he wipes his forehead.

The Sun Will Not Stop

Another hand will turn
the coffeemill at the window,
the sun will not stop.

Che incredibile mattino

Che incredibile mattino,
fuma la lingua ai cani
e Silvestro mi sta vicino.
Io non distinguo più il suono
delle campane: Sant'Antonio
o San Giacomo . . . Siamo in fondo alla valle
come in fondo ad un lago.

What an Incredible Morning

What an incredible morning,
steam's rising from the dogs' tongues
and Sylvester stays close to me.
I can't tell the sound
of bells anymore, St. Anthony's
St. James's . . . We're at the bottom of the valley
as if at the bottom of a lake.

Il cane di Lazzaro

Tu sei solo nella notte,
Cammini senza lasciare traccia.
Tu passi senza lasciare odore
Tra i neri tralci di rose
Che m'insanguinano la faccia.
Tu sei un'ombra, le tue spalle
Sono più leggere più vane
Dell'ombra delle farfalle
Sulle acque.

Saprò trovarti col fiuto
Oltre le rosee riviere,
Udrò il tuo corno di soprassalto.
Ti portavo all'aurora
Il primo saluto del giorno,
L'odore di timo sul muso.

Io ti portavo in bocca
I pesci dalle secche riviere,
Le folaghe ferite tra le felci.
Il tuo sangue era più veloce
Delle mie gambe, la tua spalla
Più forte della sbarra
Dove il fiume perde la voce.
Bello e fiero, tu eri
Nuovo da ogni lato
E dritto come le penne
Dello sparviero fucilato.

Lazarus's Dog

Alone in the night,
you walk without leaving a trace,
passing without leaving a scent
through the black rosebriars
that bloody my face.
You're a shadow, your shoulders
lighter, emptier
than the shadows of butterflies
on water.

I'll know how to find you sniffing
beyond the rose-colored shores,
I'll hear your horn all of a sudden.
I used to bring you at dawn
the first greeting of the day,
muzzle smelling of thyme.

I brought you fish
from the dry shores in my mouth,
coots wounded in the ferns.
Your blood ran faster than my legs,
your shoulder stronger that the weir
where the river looses its voice.
Handsome and proud, you were new
from every side, and straight
as a shot hawk's feathers.

About the Translation

'I used to write a poem in a flash, fifteen minutes, the canonical length set by the impressionists to paint a landscape. And I wasn't just writing descriptions, even of the transcendantal kind. I could easily write a book in a week and then forget about it. In ten days I wrote *18 Poesie*; about two years later in a few weeks *I Campi Elisi*. the final exploit [in French in the original] was *Cineraccio* in the last months of 1959. Haste or hemorrhage? By patiently applying myself I wouldn't have been able to coax a spider from his hole. Just the same I admired some of the great masters, Monsignor Della Casa who spent a whole season on a most beautiful winter sonnet, Paul Valery who filed the nails of the *Jeune Parque* for several years. I never took seriously criticism based on variants. Even the miracles of the slight corrections made by Leopardi on his manuscripts have not convinced me: I do not see a chasm between infinite and interminable spaces, between do you remember and do you recall of "A Silvia." I had to work like a blacksmith, be satisfied with a few precise hammerblows. Every game, a bet. Anyone wishing to look at my papers would find that today the coup de foudre is outside my strategy, poetry no longer meets me halfway. I have to search for it as one searches for mushrooms. Soon or later I won't find it' (Sinisgalli, quoted on the jacket of *Il passero e il lebbroso*, Mondadori, 1970).

All the poems in this collection of translations are, with a few exceptions, from *Vidi le muse* (1943), which subsumes several of Leonardo Sinisgalli's early chapbooks, including *18 Poesie* and *I Campi Elisi*, and belongs to the period when he wrote a poem in a flash. *Vidi le muse*, published by Mondadori in the series *I poeti dello specchio*, which includes Cardarelli, Quasimodo, Ungaretti, and Montale, is a collection of lyrics in which the image, quick, lively, leaping in its intuitive connections, is dominant. An architecture, a geometry of images. Sinisgalli, a man who saw no paradox in being a poet and an engineer, a poet and an art director for industrial firms such as Pirelli and Olivetti, used the image as the bridge connecting all these worlds together, as the way to reconcile and humanize. Some of his ads — the rose in the inkwell, the story of language — became classics in the field of advertising, and during the last twenty years of his life he had several exhibits and one-man shows of paintings, and ink and pastel drawings. All of his writing is enlivened by metaphor and by unusual analogies. He was able to see Piazza del Popolo in Rome, through which he walked many times every day, as 'a superb vase'; to see connections between Mallarme's flower and geometry (Sinisgalli, *Promenades Architecturales*, 72 and 22 respectively). Geometry was something pure and skeletal like Mallarme's flower, which was 'une fleur quelconque,' any flower, just as in geometry one may starts at any point to demonstrate a proof.

As a young man Sinisgalli was in love with numbers, a love that gave him ecstatic joy, and which he transferred to words as he discovered their multifaceted nature, more intriguing, more mysterious and magical than numbers. His early poems bear the imprint of his first love in their symmetrical structure. The image, though, remains the chief bearer of meaning in all of his poetry, even in the epigrams of his later years. At that point in his life any utterance becomes emblematic.

Because of this, I strove to reproduce the image and its relative connections faithfully, mindful of its correspondances, enhancing it if it became blurred in the translation. I do not believe in transposing the cultural setting. A stone hut does not become a clapboard shack; an open air threshing ground does not get moved inside a mid-western barn. Such actions constitute a kind of cultural colonialism, and just the opposite of what I feel the experience of translation should be — an encounter with others, despite our limitations of understanding and language barriers. In addition, I don't feel that this kind of transposing can be done consistently throughout a body of work, and the results are aesthetically confused. If anachronistic could be applied to place and culture, I would use the term.

But what does one do when something quite commonplace in the original is outside the experience of the American reader? For example, in 'Passionflower' one line speaks of 'holm oaks,' and another refers to 'an evergreen leaf.' If one does not know that holm oaks are evergreen, the connection is lost, and with it a correspondance to a certain feeling or state of being. In this instance, my experience was that here no one had any idea what this oak looked like, and that most assumed the kind they knew. Even the dictionary did not tell of the quality that was salient for this poem. I had to re-establish the connection between the shrub/small tree and the leaf, and since the latter is not only evergreen but shaped like a holly's, and like the holly an ilex, I decided to use holly. Associations with Christmas, etc. were not a problem in this lyric. The holly can be a shrub or a tree, its leaves are evergreen and have a shape similar to the holm oak, but also, and this is important to me, it can be found in both places. I felt that it was inappropriate to use 'live oak,' which is only found in the U.S. and has, besides, connotations of a lush semi-tropical South, and that to use notes would unnecessarily burden these short poems. In *Light Without Motion*, my traslation of Giorgio Chiesura's *La zona immobile*, in one poem I substituted geese for ducks, mainly because of the sound, but also because of the associations. Chiesura agreed with me that the change of bird did not matter. The sign remained the same. Both species fly south 'in triangles or alone.' In addition, the note of longing that I achieved with the sound of the word 'geese' would have been missing in the more literal translation. 'Puzzola', in Sinisgalli's 'September's New Moon,' a European polecat, a kind of weasel, became 'weasel' when I found out that a polecat is a skunk here, an animal found only on this continent. The poem needed an animal that stole eggs. The signs of the interior landscape as well as the signs expressive of the times and place, have to be maintained. We are entering these times and places through the consciousness of a person who belonged to them, who was shaped by them.

Both the dominant use of the image and of parallel structure recall oriental poetry. Having written the haiku, as well as used it in my classes, I immediately saw a resemblance which was later confirmed by a study by the critic Renato Aymone (*Per troppi giorni uguali. Poeti Italiani del '900*. Napoli: Edizioni Scientifiche Italiane, 1984, 111-112). He noticed a connection to the haiku, and also to the Chinese lyric, maybe through Mallarmé, and, though he found no model or text source, and no external evidence, he convincingly demonstrated his observations by lifting many two-line or three-line haiku out of Sinisgalli's poems, complete with kigo — the word that's the sign of the season. Sinisgalli's attempt to crystallize the moment into an image — 'a living sign/your cigarette's burning tip,' 'and their voices remain in mid-air, thin,' 'a fish kindles in the glass bowl' — as well as the unfolding of days, from dawn to dusk to dawn, the wheeling of stars, the constant motion that threatens to 'wind everything in its circle' seems to conform to the inner landscape, the spirit of the haiku, even when at odds with the three-line, five-seven-five syllable count.

The parallel structure as well is oriental rather than biblical. There is some repetition of sound, but not of lines, only a symmetrical structuring of elements, especially in his early poems. Occasionally this made the English version awkward. When the staccato seemed too pronounced, much more so than in the Italian, I modified it with a dependent clause.

The repetition of sound consisted of rhymes or near rhymes, sometimes at the end and sometimes in the middle of the line, but of no rhyme schemes. He writes a free verse full of endesyllabic lines, but consciously frustrates traditional expectactions.

Rhyming being so easy in Italian and so difficult in English, I have only done it when it seemed effortless, never changing the image to achieve it, but often substituting near rhymes, or consonance and assonance. And I never added words or inverted the syntax, things that would have been noticeable in a short lyric which is not humorous or satyrical. Humor has more punch in English with meter and rhyme, and, because of this, it's understandable if other things become subordinate to them.

I was guided by Sinisgalli in rendering the world of signs created by him, and in choosing diction equivalent to the original. Unlike Montale, with whom he has been compared for embodying feeling and thought in concrete images, he uses everyday language, free of archaic and/or pseudopoetic words. No native Italian needs a special glossary or even a dictionary to read Sinisgalli. What difficulties there are lie in the density of the landscape of signs, the correspondances to states of being, and the economy of language. I have kept the diction simple, by avoiding charged language, and cognates, which even when they don't change the denotation inevitably change the level of usage and, therefore, the connotation, aware that changes of this kind would constitute a distortion of the original voice.

I was careful, though, not to adhere to the syntax of the Italian. It's sheer folly to translate line by line from an inflected to an uninflected language. One may be able to do this from one romance language to another, but not from a romance language into English. I have not felt bound, either, to translate a word the same way in every instance. The *dolce* in *dolce rumore, dolcissime ingiurie, dolci tacchi, rosa dolce, dolce compagno, dolce provincia* became *soft, sweet, gentle, muted, dear, mild*. Being consistent would have resulted in mistranslations and in rather flabby lines. In addition, I recognize an arbitrary element in the whole process. Since I am making a new poem in English, not providing a trot or an interlinear translation for someone who's studying the Italian language or the culture through the language, the finished product has to sound natural and as effortless as I can make it, and as poignant. In the end I too have to ask of the new poem, 'Will the ecstacy of a fly in the sun,/ the eye of the indifferent hunter/remain in these words?' ('Where the Souls of Dogs Bark Softly.')

One way I test my translations is to read them silently moving from one to the other and back again, and I am satisfied only when the experience comes across without the language, in either version, calling undue attention to itself.

Sinisgalli wrote: 'The poet is the author of a single book that starts with the first poem and ends with the last. There is no break between one book and the next. The titles of the various collections are divisions for the sake of convenience like the names of country places on a map: a hedge, a row of stones, a brook are enough to create a difference between adjacent properties' (*Dimenticatoio,* 7-8) It is this kind of seamlessness that I aim for between the original and the translation. I know that it must sound impossible and presumptuous, probably the whole task is, but translation requires the same strategies one uses in making an original poem. In the end, despite all the careful attention to detail given the original, it's my word choices, my sense of rhythm, my own intuitive leaps that determine the poem in English. It's my critical sense that I have to rely on. The poem has to seem 'right' to me.

But this is as far as you can get from one final, or, from the only 'correct' rendering. At this point the process is not very different from the process of writing an original poem. More than one version may feel right, but, as you do with an original poem, you settle on a version to make public, reserving the right to change your mind. Eventually, though, you have to abandon any particular poem, to leave it behind, and go on to the next thing.

Biographical Notes on Leonardo Sinisgalli

1908 Born March 9 at Montemurro (Lucania, the setting for Carlo Levi's *Christ Stopped at Eboli*) to Vito Sinisgalli (1878-1953) and Carmela Lacorazza (1882-1943) third of seven children, but 'firstborn' son. His father, a tailor, like many southern Italian men had to go to America to work in order to support such a large family, to Brooklyn, NY, and Barranquilla, Colombia, two trips, one in the nineteenth century and one in the twentieth, leaving the first time when L.S. was only three. He came back to his hometown in 1922 and raised grapes and other crops (see the poem 'To My Father').

1918 At the end of WWI, and when he was only nine, he left his hometown, never to live there again, and started formal pre-university training in Caserta, transferring later to Benevento (near Naples) to attend a technical institute, still pre-university.

1922 His father came back from America and the family moved from the house above the 'fosso', (the ditch or hollow of 'Libritti,' the deep ravine that's behind his house, to which he makes reference in his stories and poems), to the 'palazzina' with a 'loggia' across the street. It was in the old house, which was empty for a while, that Sinisgalli started to write using a corner of an upstairs room as a study. I saw his house and his 'study' when I visited

Montemurro in 1989. On the outside wall, a narrow marble slab bears his name, and a large one, the poem 'I fanciulli battono le monete rosse.'

1925 Having made top grades in everything, he registered at the University of Rome, majoring in math, his passion when he was young and a source of 'ecstasy,' but graduating in engineering. He had the chance to join Enrico Fermi as one of the young men who would usher in the atomic age, but turned to poets and painters instead. He was a friend of Arnarldo Beccaria, Libero De Libero, and Scipione. In Rome he met Ungaretti in the Caffè Aragno.

1931 Did his military service. Was trained as an artillery officer on horseback.

1934 Encouraged by Zavattini to enter a contest of prose and poetry, he took first prize for poetry. Attilio Bertolucci won second prize for poetry, and Alfonso Gatto took a prize for prose. Ungaretti, Bacchelli and Palazzeschi were part of the jury. The winning poems were panned by the critics, one of whom treated him as a plagiarist of Quasimodo.

1934 Unable to find work, he spent the summer and fall at home (in Montemurro), and almost decided not to go back to Milan. He wrote his *Quaderno di geometria* and several of his *18 Poesie.*

1936 Urged by his friends, he went back to Milano where he soon found work in industry, in the world of graphics and publicity.

1936 *18 Poesie* was published. He felt he had found his voice, a poetic discourse between poetry and anti-poetry which would be his chief 'weapon.'

1938 He became art director for Olivetti of Milano, a position he was very proud of.

1938 He had great success in his work. Many of his ads – the rose in the inkwell, the story of writing – have become classics.

1938-40 *Poesie* and *I Campi Elisi* came out.

1940 Drafted, served in Piemonte and Sardinia. 'Santo Stefano' (there are two poems by that name) is in Piemonte, Abbasanta (in 'The Sky's Flickering') is in Sardinia.

1940 In Rome he met Giorgia De Cousandier who became his companion and later his wife. He raised Filippo, her youngest child by a previous marriage, as his own.

1943 *Vidi le muse* was published by Mondadori and he joined Cardarelli, Quasimodo, Ungaretti, Montale as a poet of *Lo Specchio*.

1944 On May 13 he was arrested in his house by the SS who had found his name in an address book of a suspect. He was dragged to the notorious prison in Via Tasso, but only stayed twenty-four hours, thanks to Georgia De Cousandier's courage and knowledge of German. When the allies got to Rome, Sinisgalli, De Cousandier, and her son Filippo were finally able to go to Montemurro. Here he found that his mother, to whom he was very close, had died nine months earlier.

1945 Settled in Rome.

1947 *I Nuovi Campi Elisi* came out.

1948 Became art director of Pirelli in Milano, and for several years traveled back and forth between Rome and Milano.

1954 Went to New York to visit his relatives.
1961 Received the Premio Etna-Taormina.
1962 Began to show his portraits and drawings in Milano and Rome.
1966 *Poesie di ieri* received the Premio Fiuggi.
1967 He had his first heart attack.
1971 He received the Premio Gubbio-Inghirami for his poetry.
1974 Had a one-man show of drawings, portraits and etchings in Milano.
1975 Was given the Premio Viareggio for *Mosche in bottiglia*, a collection of poems, and the Premio Basilicata (another name for Lucania) for *Un disegno di Scipione e altri racconti*, a prose work.
1978 Premio Vallombrosa for *Dimenticatoio*, poetry.
1978 His wife died.
1979 Exhibited his pastel drawings at Matera.
1980 Exhibited his pastels in Rome.
1981 Second one-man show of watercolors, ink and pastel drawings at the 'Millennio,' Rome.
1981 He died on January 31 and was buried in the 'Elysian Fields' of Montemurro.

About the Translator

Rina Ferrarelli was born in the province of Cosenza, Calabria, Italy, and emigrated to the United States at the age of fifteen. She attended Carlow College and Duquesne University, and has been teaching English and translation studies at the University of Pittsburgh, Pittsburgh, Pa. She is married to Foster Provost and has three children.

She is a poet and translator. *Dreamsearch* (Malafemmina Press, 1992) is her first chapbook of original poetry, and *Light Without Motion* (Owl Creek Press, 1989), her first collection of translations, a sequence of *poesie-racconti* about WWII from the Italian of Giorgio Chiesura. She was awarded the Italo Calvino Prize from the Columbia University Translation Center, and a National Endowment for the Arts grant.

Printed in March 1997 by
VEILLEUX
ON DEMAND PRINTING INC.
in Boucherville, Quebec